Coloring Adventures with Arthur and Throcky

A Coloring Buddy Book for Grownups and Kids

Coloring Adventures with Arthur and Throcky
A Coloring Buddy Book for Grownups and Kids

ISBN-13: 978-1519352026
ISBN-10: 1519352026
©2014-2015 Pance Productions
and Karen DeCrane

There are many types of licensed use available under copyright laws. Rather than go into a dry legalese rundown of what sort of copyright license I grant you, I'll keep it simple.

Here's what you can do:
• Make unlimited copies of the pages in this book for your own use. You can print those copies on your own choice of paper as many times as you wish.
• Display, gift or sell the finished work where ever you wish. It would be nice if you mentioned me or the book, but it's ok if you don't.

Here's what you can't do:
• Sell, gift or display uncolored pages - anywhere. If your favorite aunt loves the work, she needs to buy the book to make her own creation.

In short, this is a collaborative work between you and me. I provide the framework for your creativity. You own that creative effort, and can do what ever you wish with colored in pages which includes having fun, coloring outside the lines and even coloring tigers with polka dots instead of stripes.

There are many benefits to coloring. It can be fun, relaxing and deeply satisfying for any age or coloring experience level. But, sharing the coloring experience with chidren or other adults usually means purchasing multiple coloring books each with it's own design theme and detail level.

Coloring Buddy coloring books are designed to be colored in by everyone, regardless of how well coloring techniques have been mastered. Simple illustrations are well suited for children or adults who just want to get back to the joys of childhood coloring.

The more intricate illustrations are perfect for the advanced colorist, with smaller details and more involved coloring areas.

Some pages are perfect for collaborative efforts, with areas that beg to be blended and enhanced by the expert colorist, yet still retaining coloring areas that even young children can enjoy and master.

No matter what your level of coloring expertise, from tiny fingered four year olds to the time worn hands of a 90 year old, you will find something to delight your creativity in the pages of a Coloring Buddy coloring book.

Sit down with your coloring sidekick and a Coloring Buddy coloring book and let the creative sharing begin!

A word about the physical properties of this book is in order. You may wonder why I haven't used perforated pages in a coloring book that is meant to be shared. In the printing world, perforating pages can be wickedly expensive. As grown-up coloring books become more and more popular, that process will probably drop in price, but for now, I choose not to include that process to keep the price of Coloring Buddy coloring books at a more affordable cost.

All is not lost, however. I've used a glue binding, that allows the pages to be easily removed. This glue melts when low heat is applied, so running a hair dryer over the binding will neatly loosen the pages. Or, you can use a straight edge to tear the pages cleanly from the book.

I hope you enjoy coloring these pages with your kids, your husband, your grandma - anyone who loves to make drawings come alive with color.

KAREN DeCRANE

Arthur, a very ordinary boy, wanted to find a friend. But Arthur was too heavy to float over his backyard fence holding a bunch of balloons.

Arthur Finds a Friend

When the bunch of balloons wouldn't work, Arthur reached into his bottomless backpack and pulled out a colorful, giant balloon with a small basket.

Arthur Finds a Friend

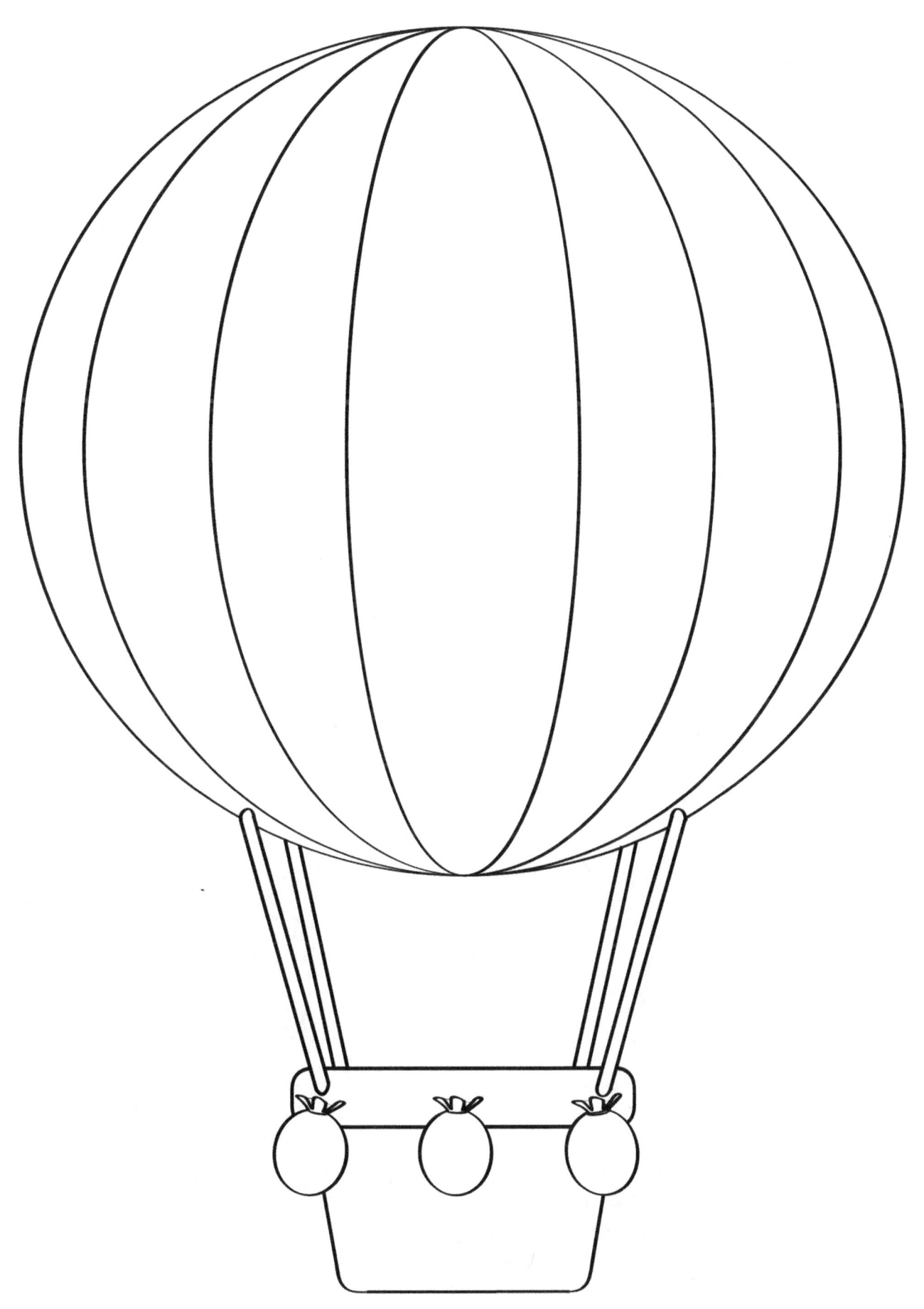

Arthur became trapped on an island as a hungry shark swam by, wanting to turn him into lunch.

Arthur Finds a Friend

Arthur's bottomless backpack held just the thing an angry snake needed to find his happy place.

Arthur Finds a Friend

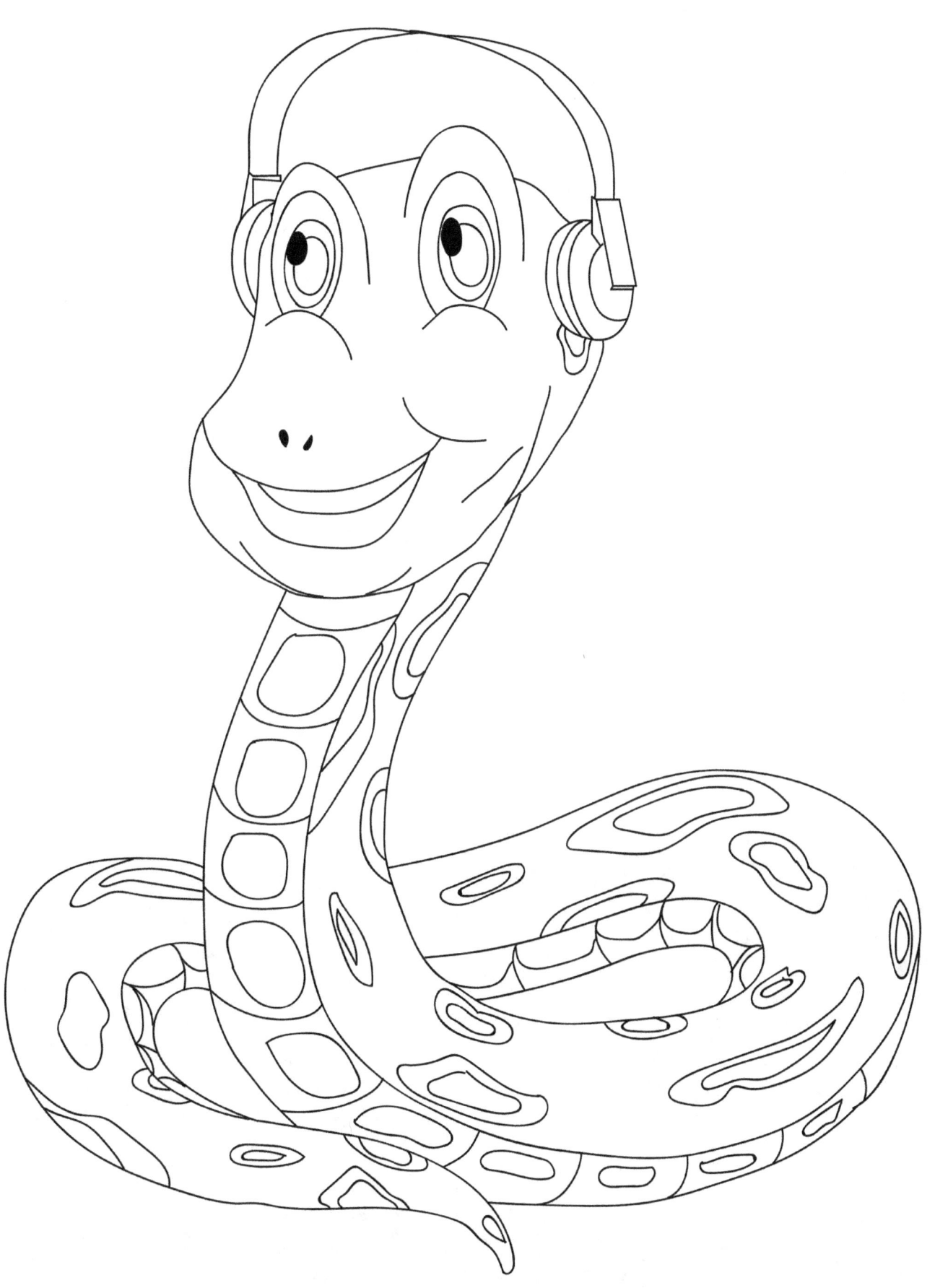

*Arthur even found a way to turn an ordinary tiger
into an extraordinary tiger.*

Arthur Finds a Friend

Arthur stood in his backyard trying to figure out how to get over the very tall fence and begin his search for a friend.

Arthur Finds a Friend

Arthur was soon sailing far above the country side in his large, colorful balloon.

Arthur Finds a Friend

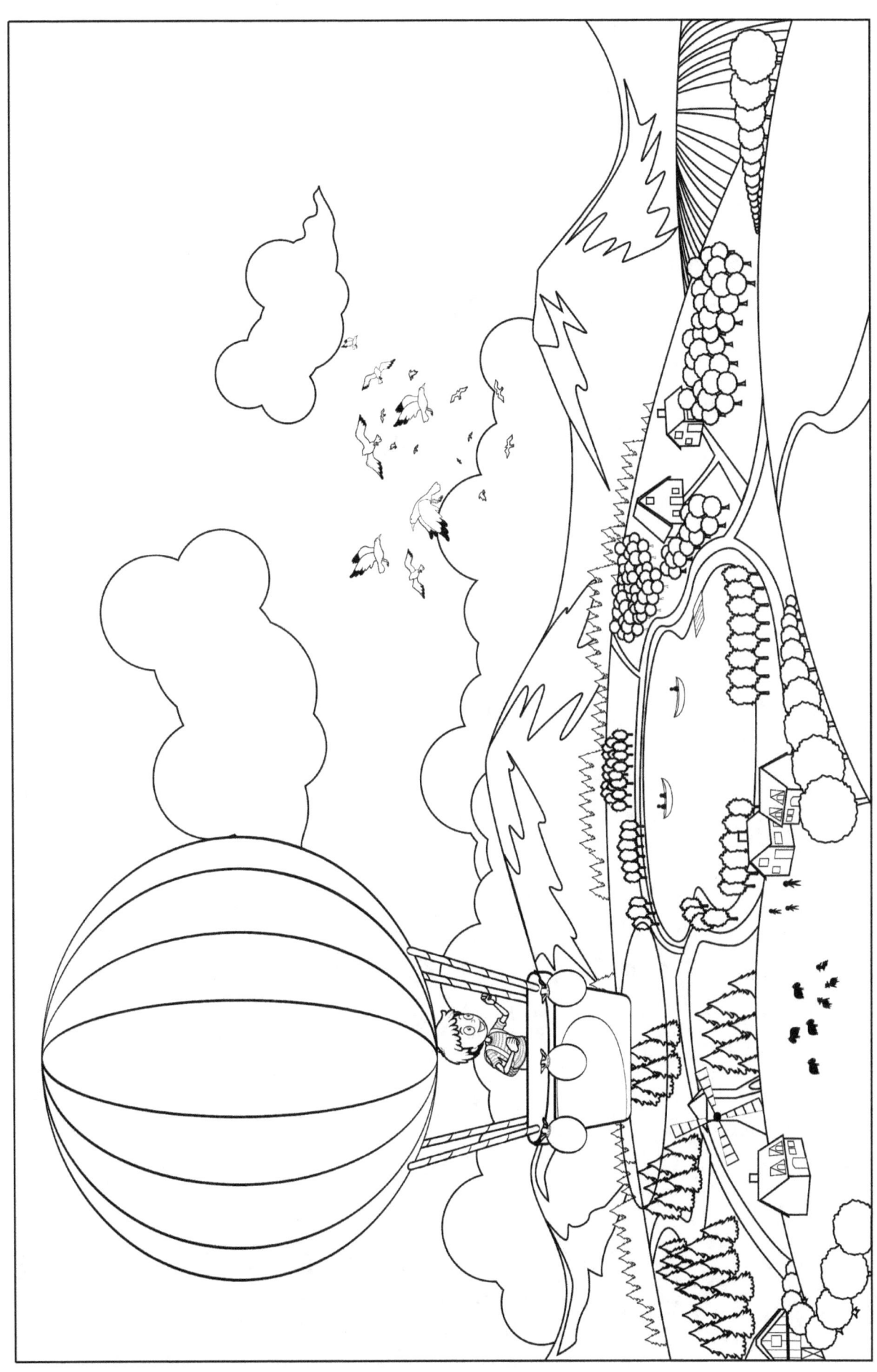

A hungry shark had plans to turn Arthur into a tasty snack, but the bottomless backpack saved the day.

Arthur Finds a Friend

*After sending the hungry shark on it's way, Arthur
found himself on a path in a magical forest .*

Arthur Finds a Friend

Arthur's bottomless backpack held just the thing an angry snake needed to find his happy place.

Arthur Finds a Friend

Snowmen have lots of snowy fun on The Island of Lost Toys in the North Pole.

Arthur and Throcky Save Christmas

Santa's elves don't just make Christmas presents, they check each one at least twice.

Arthur and Throcky Save Christmas

Rupert, the lost Polar Bear arrived at the North Pole, hoping to find some new friends to play with.

Arthur and Throcky Save Christmas

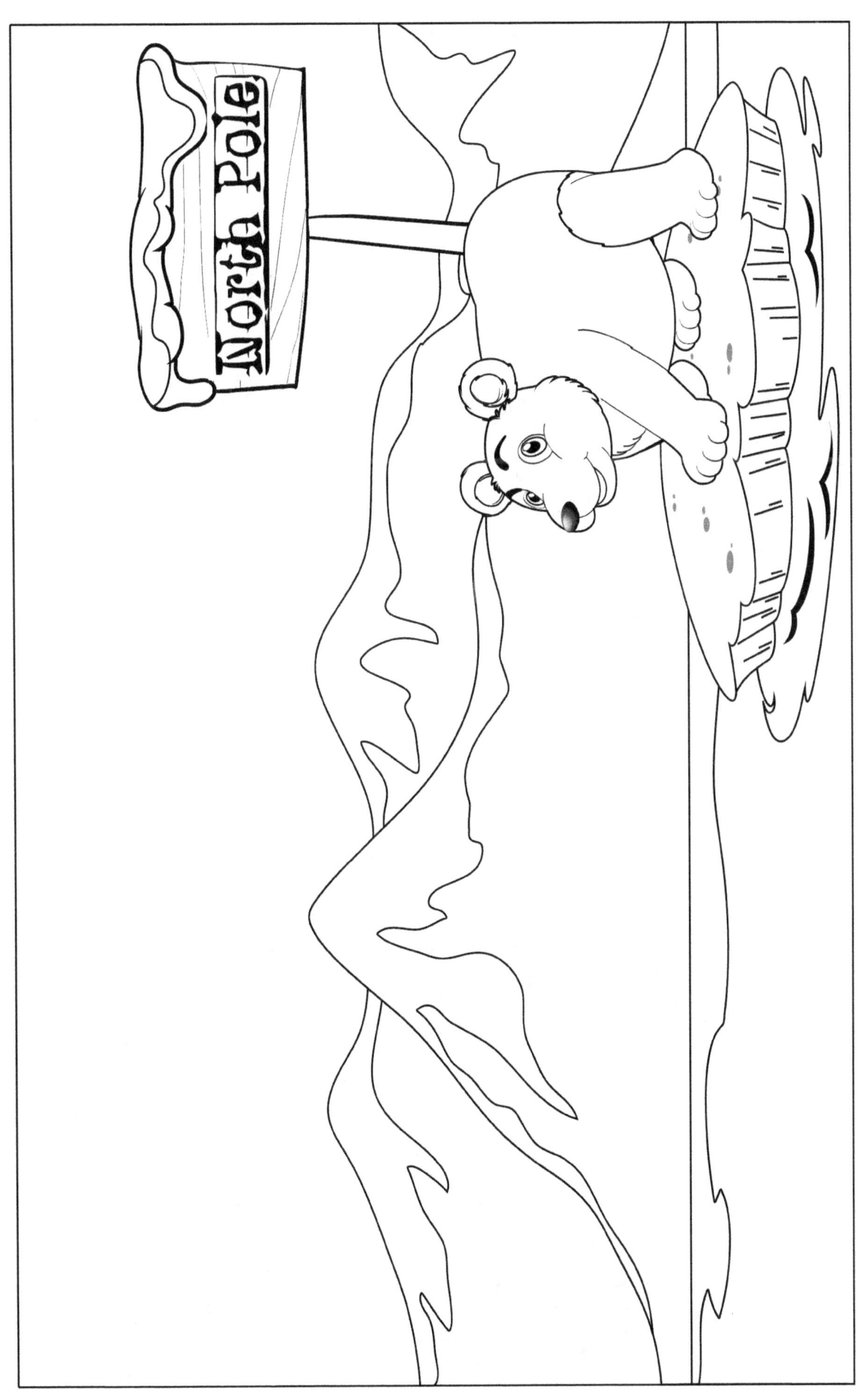

Santa seems to be everywhere at the North Pole as he gets ready for his big night.

Arthur and Throcky Save Christmas

Santa Throcky helps lighten the load for Santa and the elves.

Arthur and Throcky Save Christmas

The peaceful North Pole village of Santa's elves won't be peaceful for long!

Arthur and Throcky Save Christmas

Santa has his list and he's checking it twice.

Arthur and Throcky Save Christmas

Busy elves create all sorts of neat toys at Santa's Christmas Workshop.

Arthur and Throcky Save Christmas

Elves whistle as they work and will find a way to make any task a fun time.

Arthur and Throcky Save Christmas

When everyone works together, Christmas can happen for children around the world.

Arthur and Throcky Save Christmas

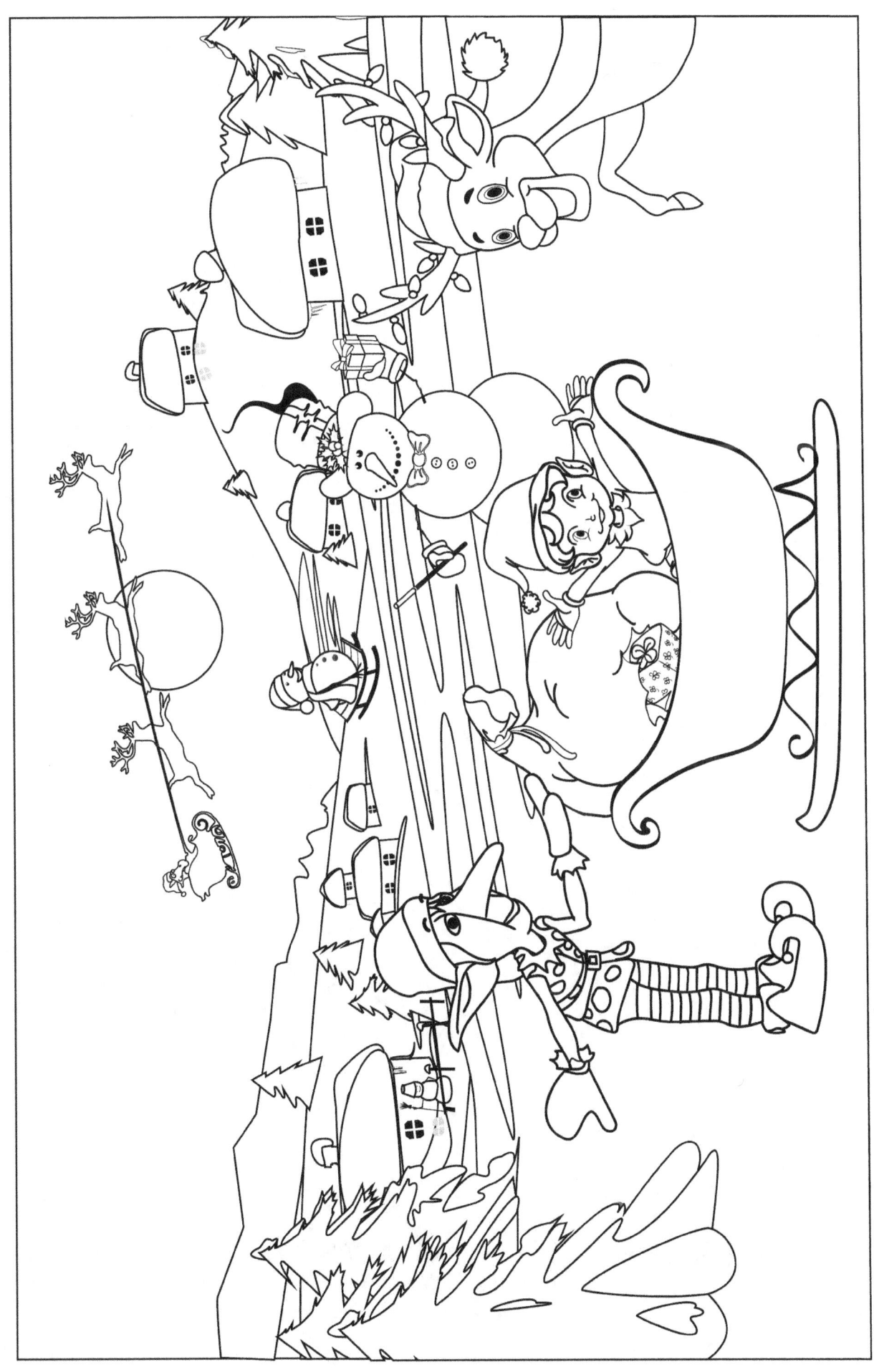

Columbus set sail in 1492 with the Nina, the Pinta and the Santa Maria. But did he land on the shores of North America?

The Explorers - Discovering America

Spanish ships were strong and sturdy and had many sails to catch the wind that drove them through the Atlantic seas.

The Explorers - Discovering America

Columbus found an island in the Carribean Sea after sailing for so many days his food and water had almost run out.

The Explorers - Discovering America

Stout, leather covered Irish boats called curraghs were used by St. Brendan to explore the lands of the North Atlantic.

The Explorers - Discovering America

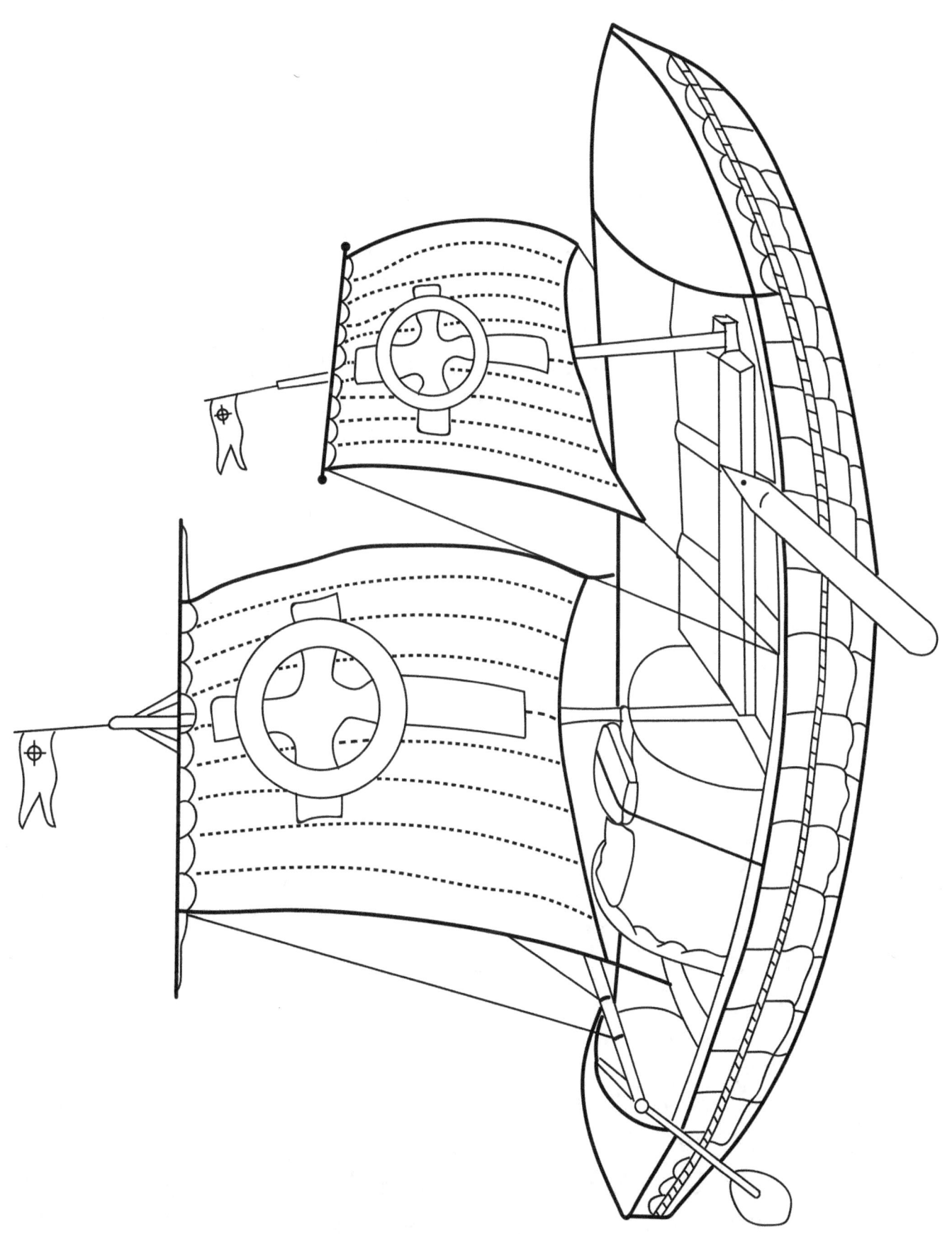

According to his journal, St. Brendan had many adventures on his journey and even rested for a time on the back of a sea monster.

The Explorers - Discovering America

The Vikings used both sails and oars to power their long boats across the cold, stormy seas.

The Explorers - Discovering America

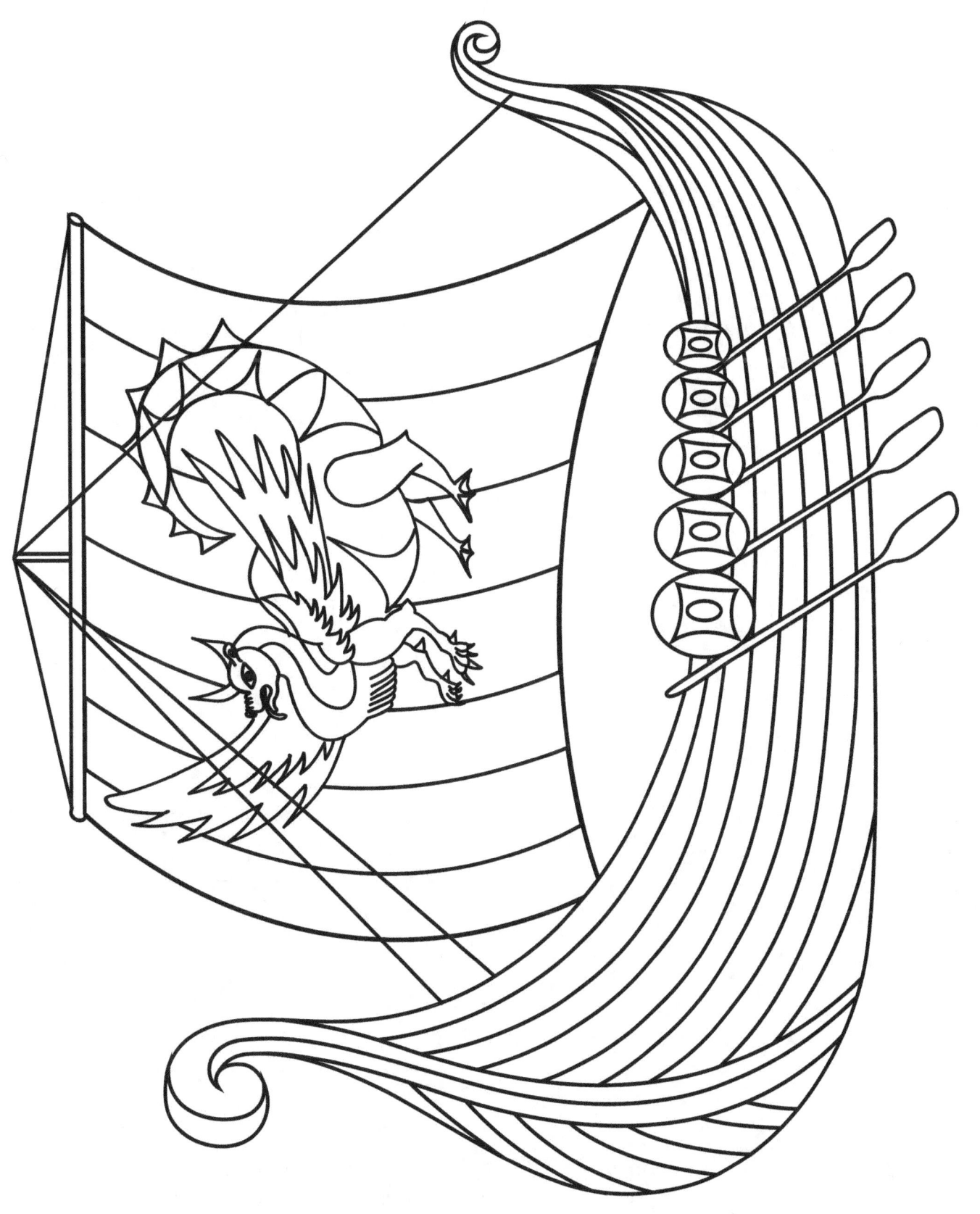

Torvald, a Viking mouse, shared stories of exploring new lands with Arthur and Throcky.

The Explorers - Discovering America

The Vikings set sail looking for lands that had strong trees for ship building and good soil for growing crops.

The Explorers - Discovering America

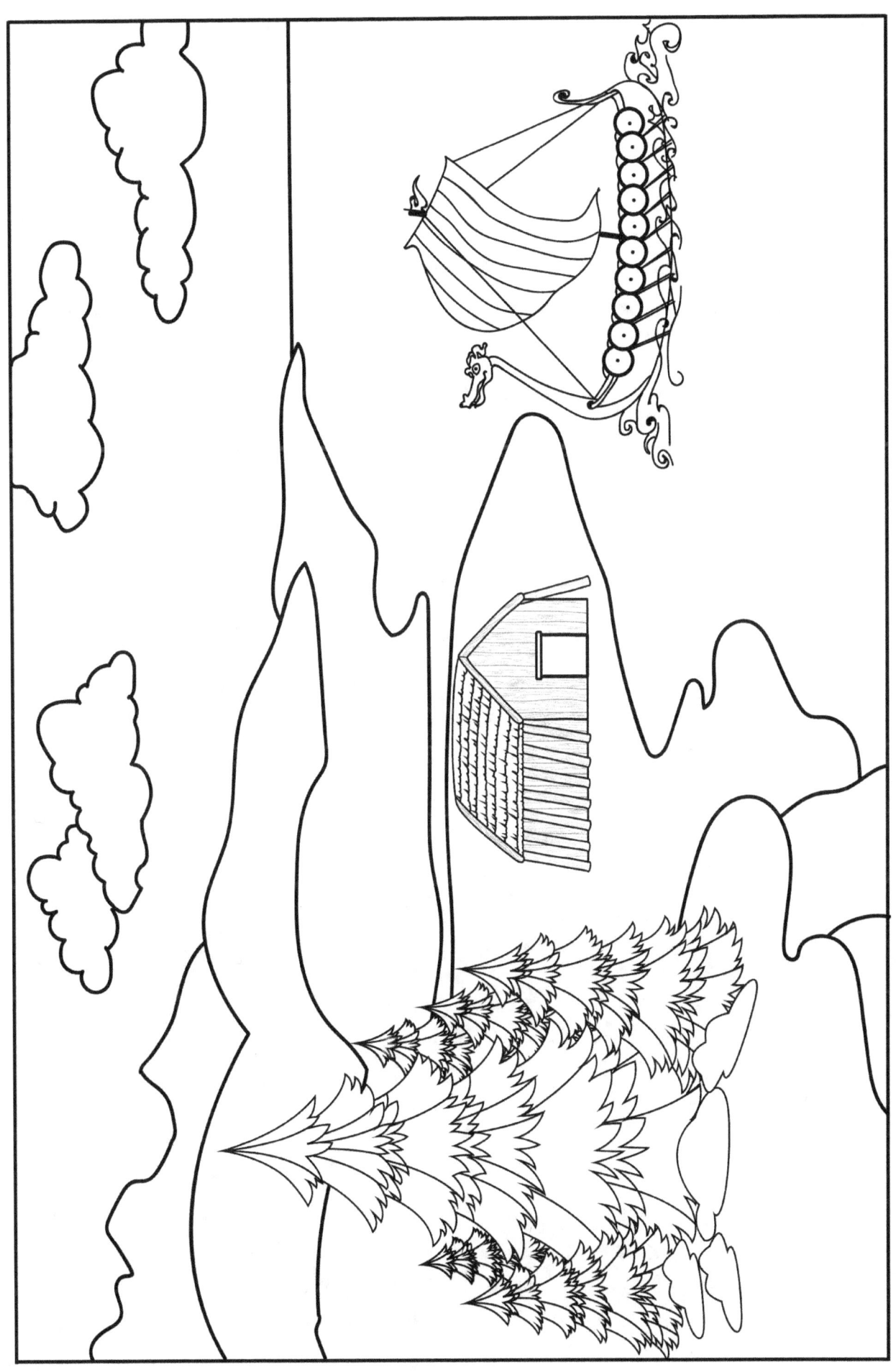

When your best friend is a time-travelling dragon, history homework becomes an interesting adventure.

The Explorers - Discovering America

With a time travelling dragon at your side, you can follow the path the early explorers took as they travelled the seas to discover America.

The Explorers - Discovering America

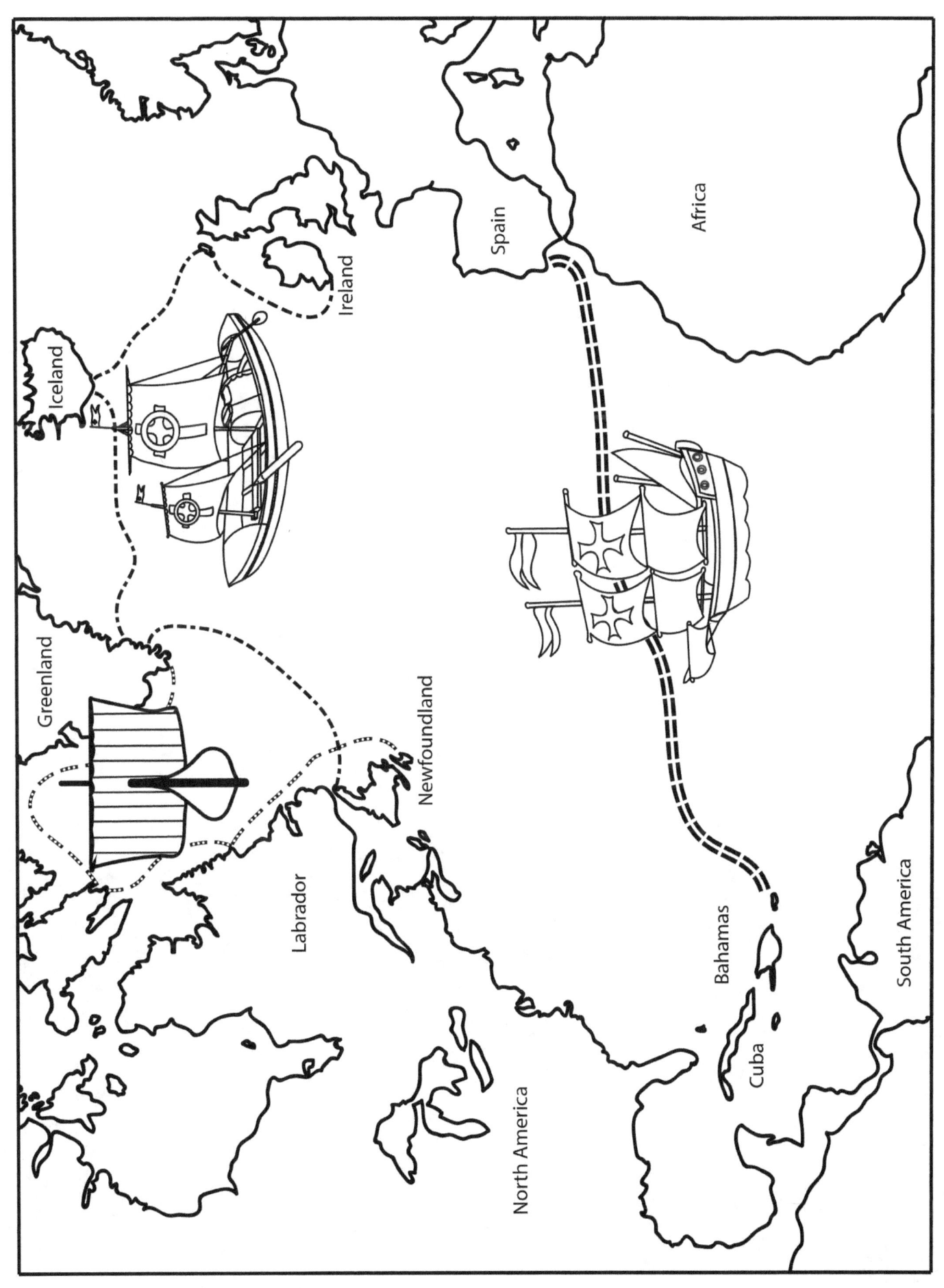